EVIDENCE THROUGH MAPS

BILL BOYLE

GENERAL EDITOR: DAVID PENROSE

COLLINS
EDUCATIONAL

INTRODUCTION

The *How Do We Know?* series is contingent on the premise that all history is based on the interpretation of evidence. In this book, children discover how to use and interpret another form of evidence, largely pictorial in presentation, through the medium of maps.

By using the different types of maps available on a given area, through a time span of several centuries, the children observe how a "historical picture" of the identifiable area develops. At the same time they are acquiring a knowledge of the sources and techniques required for a similar investigation of their own area.

The point is made firmly throughout the book that whether you live in an old-established part of town, or on a new housing estate, there is history to your area. The past may be hidden, but if you know how to look for the clues on the maps, it will be revealed.

Bill Boyle is Deputy Headteacher of Manor Junior School, Birkenhead. He is the author of several educational books and has many years teaching experience.

© 1988 Bill Boyle

First published in Great Britain 1988 by
Collins Educational
8 Grafton Street, London W1X 3LA

Reprinted 1989

Typeset by Scribe Design, Gillingham, Kent
Printed and bound by Hollen Street Press, Berkshire

ISBN 0 00 315414 9

CONTENTS

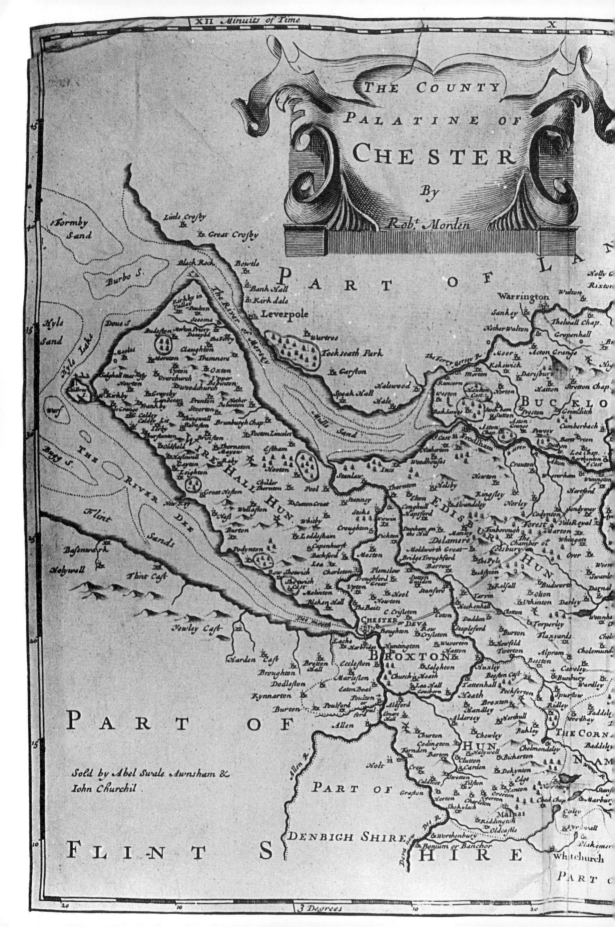

Why maps?

As you have seen in other books in this series, historians collect much evidence through studying documents. In this book, you will see how maps can be very useful sources of evidence for a history detective. If we read them correctly, maps can help us to discover what a place was like in the past, and how it has changed over the years.

There are different types of maps that can be used to find clues about the past. Here are four of the more important ones.

1 There are many **early maps** of particular areas drawn up hundreds of years ago. This is part of Robert Morden's map of 1695 showing the County Palatinate of Chester. Notice how this early map does not have roads marked on it, but does have *symbols* for forests, hills and mills.

● Draw any symbols that you can see.

Left: 1695 map of Cheshire

2 About 150 years ago, thousands of **tithe maps** such as the one below were drawn up. *Surveyors* drew up maps of the parishes throughout the country to decide how much *tithe* (church tax) the landowners needed to pay. These maps have a lot of information on them and are very useful to the history detective. On this section of the 1840 map of Barton in Cheshire, see how the buildings and fields are all numbered. Why do you think this was done?

1840 map of Barton, Cheshire

3 Ordnance Survey maps are the most accurate plans of an area. They are the official maps made of an area by the government and have been used since 1801 by anyone wishing to study the details of any part of the country. They are very useful to historians searching for evidence of the past.

They were first drawn up for the English soldiers fighting in Scotland after the Jacobite rebellion of 1745–6. The maps were to help the soldiers find their way quickly around the Scottish countryside if there was another rebellion. General William Roy was the man responsible for making these first maps. He was the first man to use a *theodolite* for surveying the areas to be mapped.

After General Roy died in 1790, his mapping work was carried on by His Majesty's Ordnance Survey. This was a part of the army which looked after the guns. Their name is still used today for the maps.

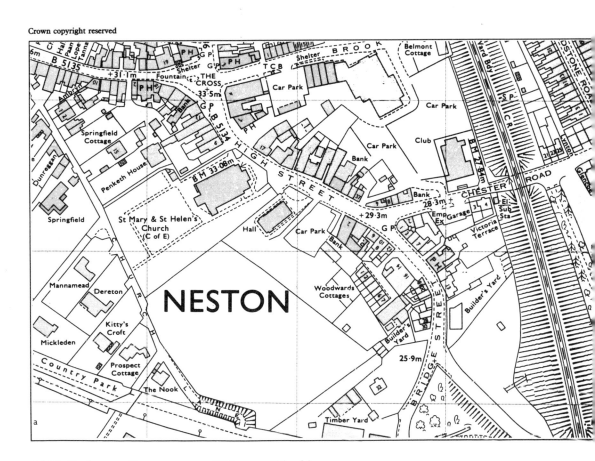

1967 Ordnance Survey map of Neston, Cheshire

4 Although not exactly a map, the **aerial photograph** taken from an aeroplane of an area can be very useful for the history detective. It lays out all the details on the ground like a map, but often shows up things that can be missed on a 'flat' plan or map.

Aerial photograph of a housing estate and an industrial estate

Understanding maps

Drawing to scale

In order to understand the information on maps, you need to learn about *scale*.

Maps have to be smaller than the areas that they *represent* or otherwise they would never fit on the pages of books! So, to be drawn accurately, maps have to be drawn to a certain size. When the *scale* has been chosen, everything on that map, must be drawn to that scale or else a village might look bigger than a city.

The scale is often shown as a *ratio*, for example 1:1 million. This means that 1 centimetre on the map is equal to 1 million centimetres (10 kilometres) on the ground. The smaller the ground distance (for example 1:500,000) the larger the scale of the map which means that there is more detail.

Look at the three maps on pages 9 and 10.

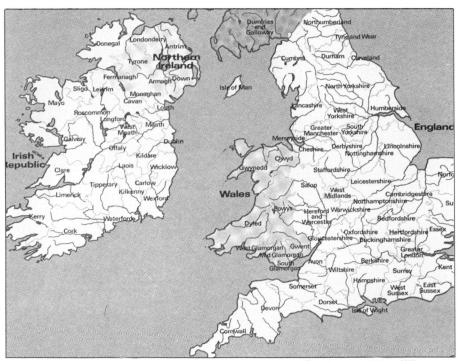

Scale – 1:6.6 million

0km   66km   132km   198km

A   British Isles

B Wales and West Midlands

Scale – 1:2.0 million

0km   20km   40km   60km

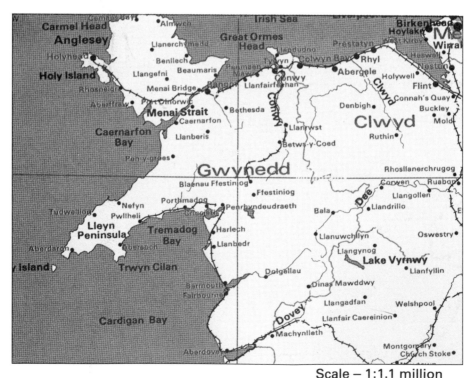

C Wales

Scale – 1:1.1 million

0km   11km   22km   33km

Although all three maps cover the same space on the page, they each show different amounts of countryside. The difference is because each map is drawn to a different scale.

● Find the scale for each map.

● Work out how many square kilometres each of the three maps covers by using the scale.

The first Ordnance Survey maps used a scale of one inch on the map to represent one mile of actual countryside. Gradually the surveyors began to draw maps to other scales. There were maps of six inches to one mile and twenty five inches for one mile. Now all Ordnance Survey maps are in *metric* measurements. The larger scale ones are ideal for studying areas in detail, for example, 1:50,000.

Map symbols

It is impossible to fit every detail about an area onto a map. In fact, maps drawn to different scales will show different amounts of detail. Why is this? To save room, *symbols* are used to represent buildings, rivers etc.

Look at the map on pages 12–13 which was made over 150 years ago.

● Has the map got a *key* for any symbols used? What word is used instead of key?

● What symbols are used in the key?

● There are other interesting things drawn on the map which could have been shown instead by symbols in the key. Make up your own key and include the symbols you would use.

● This map is entitled the *Hundred* of Wirral. Do some research for yourself to find out the meaning of this word.

Overleaf: The Hundred of Wirral

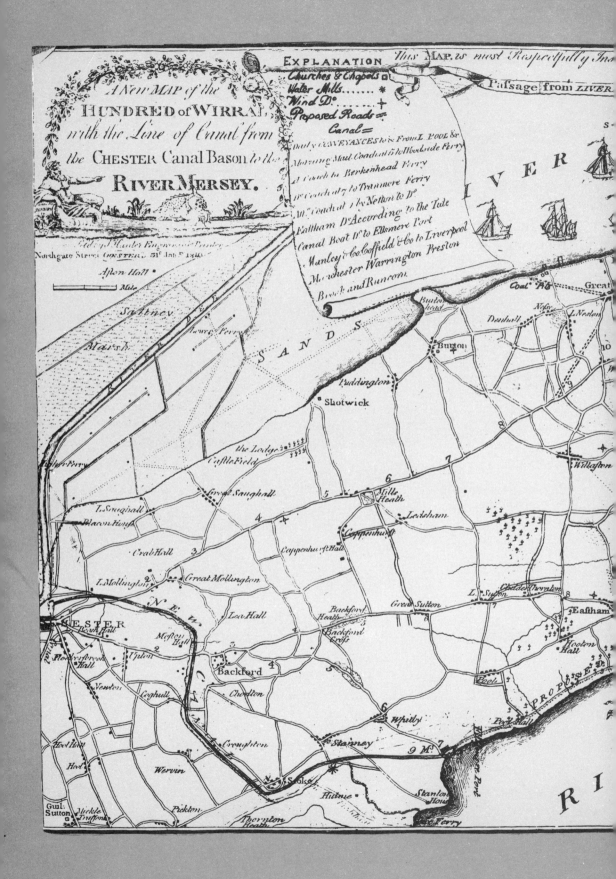

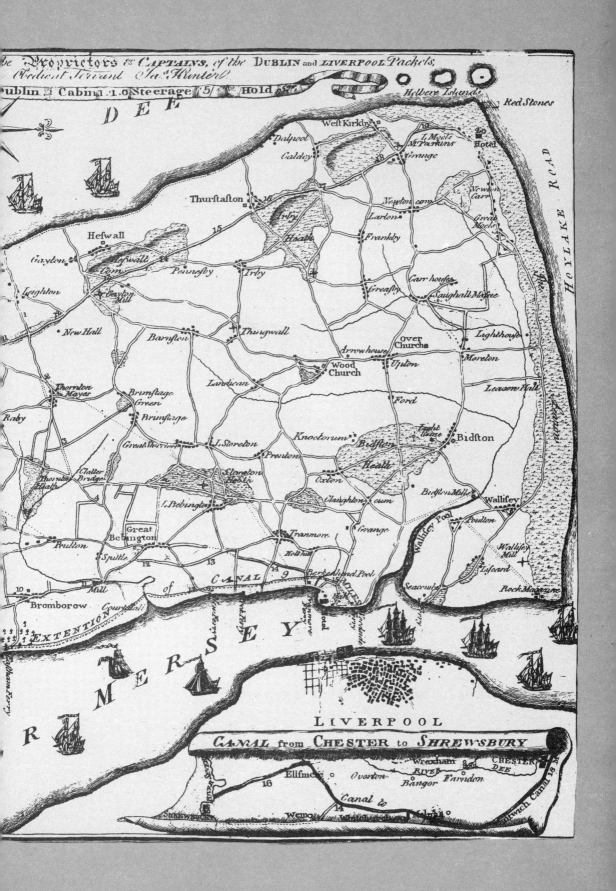

Ordnance Survey maps use a set of symbols called *conventional signs* for their maps. Below are the main signs used.

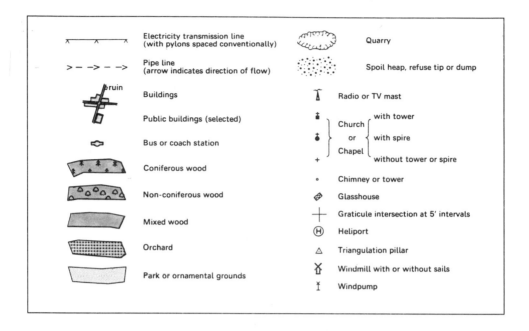

Look at the map based on the Ordnance Survey on page 15. Make a list of all the conventional signs that you can find on it.

- Which city is shown on the map?

- List any historical symbols you can find.

- How are schools shown? How many can you find?

- How many farms can you find?

- What is the airport called? Design a symbol for it.

Look at a large scale (1:50,000) Ordnance Survey map of your district. Reading the symbols will help you gather information about your area.

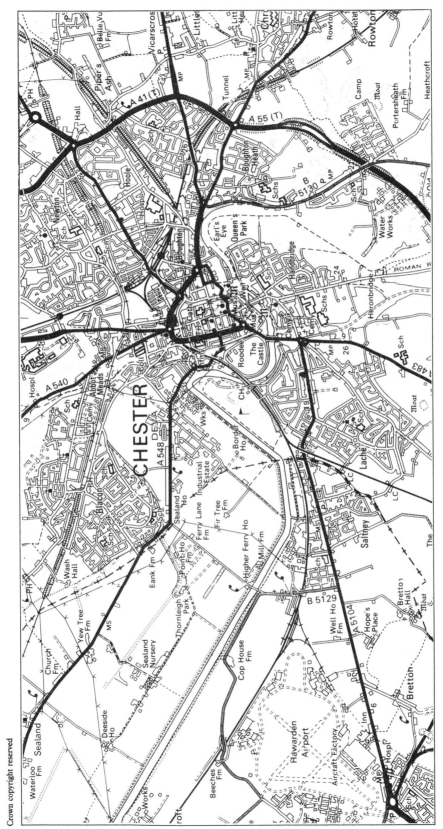

Map of Chester based on Ordnance Survey

Where we live

Here are Paula and Colin. They are in the same class at Manor School, Birkenhead in Merseyside. They are working with their teacher on a project about the history of where they live.

The children began by making their own maps of the area around their school. They marked in any buildings of historical interest.

Paula

Here is Paula's map.

N ←

Key
- ⊟ house
- ⊠ masionette
- ❀ Bullring
- = road
- ▬ school
- ⊠ Pub
- ⊡ flats
- ❀ woods
- ‡ bridge
- — seat
- ◎ Lighthouse
- ⚙ Windmill
- ⊞ observatory

Paula's map gives you some clues to the sort of area she lives in.

● Do you think she lives in the centre of town or in an old village or on a modern housing estate? What evidence is there for your answer?

Paula's teacher brought in sections from the 1978 Ordnance Survey map for the area to help the children locate their own homes (see below). They also used these maps to compare the accuracy of the maps they had drawn.

In the map section shown on page 17, Paula was able to identify her home at 47 Ford Towers.

● Find Paula's address on the map. What do you discover about her home?

● What further evidence can you find from this Ordnance Survey section about the type of area that Paula lives in? Look at the *pattern* of the street lay-out.

● What do you think the buildings in Ford Precinct might include?

● Which members of the *community* might live in Feltree House and Esher House?

Ask your local librarian to show you a recent large scale Ordnance Survey map for your area so that you can point out where you live.

Colin

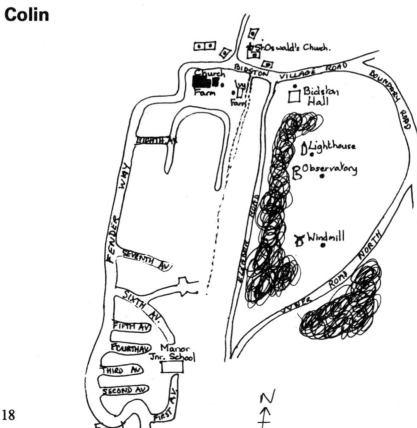

Colin's map shows his home, Church Farm in Bidston. You can work out his *route* from home to school. He has marked with a 'dot' the buildings of historical interest.

● Make a list of the buildings of historical interest.

● Put a tick by the ones which Paula has also marked on her map on page 16.

Look carefully at the children's maps. What clues can you find which suggest that Colin lives in an area that was built before Paula's?

Historical buildings

Look at this map. Some of the historical buildings shown on the maps drawn by Paula and Colin are marked here.

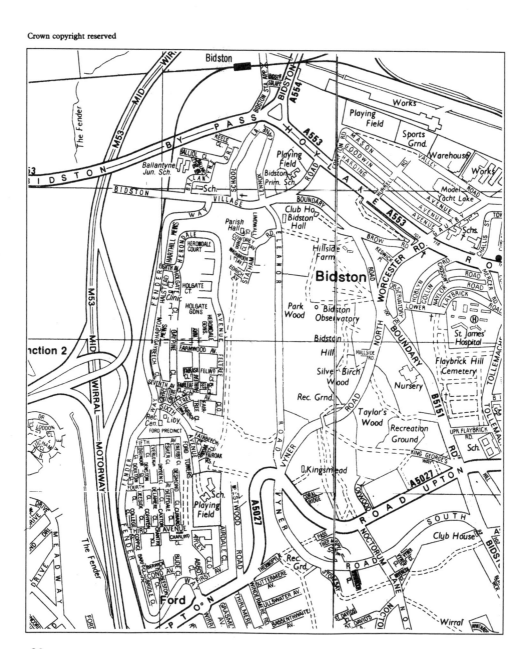

- How many historical buildings can you spot?

- What buildings appear on both the children's maps but not on the map on page 20?

- What is the high ground called shown on the map?

- What is one building marked on the map which neither Colin nor Paula have shown on their maps?

- What do you think it is used for?

Colin bought into school this old postcard of Bidston Church, which his grandfather had given to him. You can locate the church on the map on page 20.

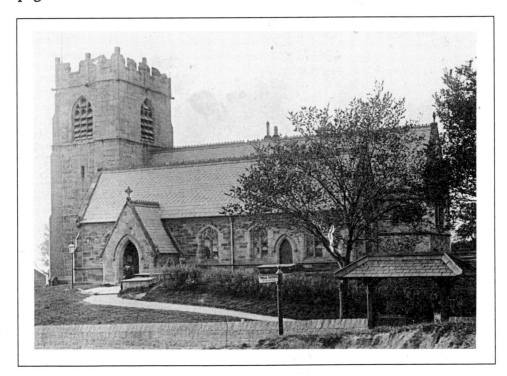

Bidston church

This gave the children the idea of looking more closely at the historical buildings which Colin's map had shown around his home in Bidston village.

They decided to draw a map of the church and the buildings around it. They gave each of the buildings a number so that they could identify them.

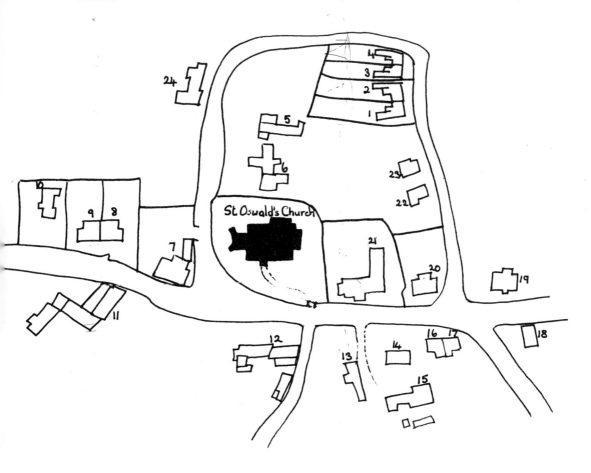

St. Oswald's Church

Making a survey

The children made a survey of the buildings that they had put on their map. They wanted to find out if different materials had been used to make the buildings in the village. They drew this *key* to help them identify easily the materials used.

Walls		Roof	
Materials	Symbol	Materials	Symbol
brick	B	thatch	TH.
stone	St.	slate	S
timber	Tm.	tiles	T
concrete	C	asphalt	A
		concrete	C
		timber	Tm.

Then the children drew up a survey sheet.

Building		Building Materials.	
no.	type	walls	roof
1	house	B	T
2	house	B	T
3	house	B	T
4	house	B	T
5	house	St	S
6	house	St.	S
7	house	St.	S
8	house	St.	S
9	house	St.	S
10	house	St.	S
11	Farm	St.	S
12	Farm	St.	S
13	house	St.	S
14	house	B	T
15	farm	St.	S
16	house	B	T
17	house	B	T
18	house	St.	S
19	house	B	T
20	house	B	T
21	house	St.	S
22	house	B	T
23	house	B.	T
24	vicarage	St.	S

● Trace the map on page 22. Use the survey sheet to find out what materials the walls of each building are made of. Choose colours to stand for each building material, for example, purple for stone. Colour your map and add a colour key.

Even though Paula lives on a modern housing estate, the maps show evidence of links with the area's history.

While studying a section of the 1975 Ordnance Survey map showing the estate, Paula notices the *One O'Clock Gun* public house marked. She passed it when she visited Colin's house and had often wondered about its unusual name.

1975 Ordnance Survey map

Paula was delighted when her grandfather showed her the old postcard shown above of the One O'Clock Gun. He told Paula that the gun used to be fired daily from nearby Bidston Hill, (see map on page 20), as a time signal to ships on the river Mersey. When the estate was built one of the public houses was named after this piece of local history.

To help you explore the history of your own area, draw maps like Paula and Colin. Use Ordnance Survey maps to collect evidence—1:1250 scale is an ideal size. Don't forget the *hidden* history that may be behind the names on the map!

Bidston Hall

Colin took this photograph of Bidston Hall which overlooks his farmhouse. In his search for information at the library he discovered a very old map. It was entitled, 'A Survey of the Manor of Bidstone in Cheshire in England belonging unto the right honourable John, Lord Kingston' and dated 1665.

Look carefully at the section below which has been redrawn.

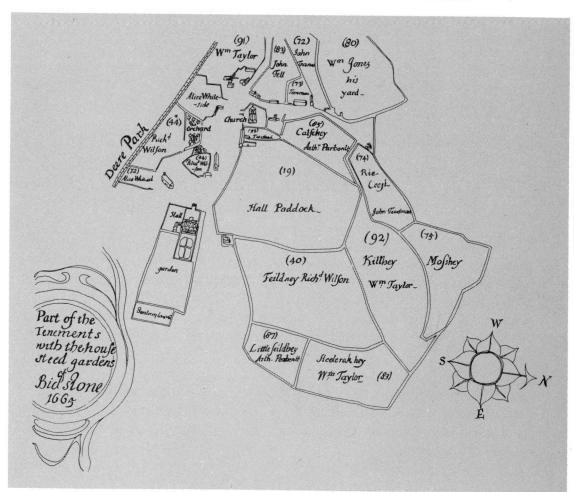

The map shows clearly that the Hall was built by 1665. Colin then compared the old map with this extract from the 1954 section of the Ordnance Survey map for the area.

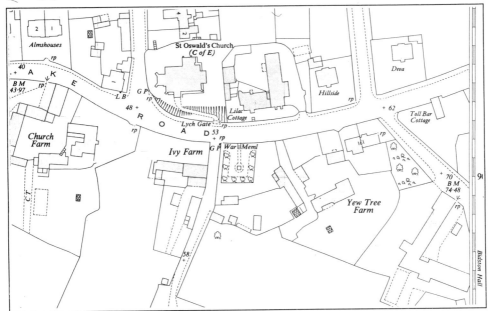

1954 Ordnance Survey map

- List the buildings you can find which are shown on both maps.

- How are the buildings represented differently on the two maps?

- Find Taylor's farm on the 1665 map. What is its name today? (Clue: Colin lives there.)

- What does the existence of the Toll Bar Cottage tell you? You can read about *tolls* in *Time and Motion*, another book in the series.

- Find the almshouses. Who would have lived in them?

- What differences do you think that 300 years have made to life in Bidston village?

Here is another redrawn map from the Kingston Survey of 1665. It shows the 'Deere Park and the meddows being part of the *Demesne* land of Bidstone 1665'.

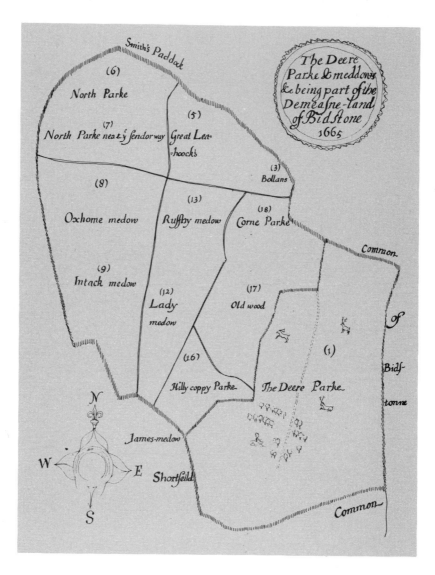

● Find out what the word *demesne* meant. Its use here is a clue to the earlier history of Bidston.

Colin was puzzled to find that there had been a Deer Park at Bidston. On investigating in the local history collection at the library he discovered that the Lord of the Manor and his guests had enjoyed hunting the deer, kept inside the Deer Park.

Colin went searching on the Hill and found remains of the wall which used to surround the Park. It is known locally as the *Penny-a-day Dyke* because the men who built it were paid a penny each day.

The Penny-a-day dyke

Search for old maps of your area. See if you can find clues to secrets of the past as Colin did.

Farming

Colin was keen to show his grandad his new map discoveries. He was delighted when grandad produced this old photograph of men working on Church Farm in the early 1900s.

- List the ways in which farming has changed today.

If you look back at the Kingston map on page 26, you will see a number of small *enclosures*. These show the tiny farms that were built on the Hill in the seventeenth century. The people who kept these farms were called *subsistence farmers*.

- Why were they called subsistence farmers?

- List the names of these farmers from the map.

- Look at the 1954 ordnance survey map on page 27. Three farms are shown there. Why do you think they survived?

Bidston Hill

From her flat on the twelfth floor of Ford Towers Paula can see many of the historical buildings on Bidston Hill. The local librarian helped her to find out more about the buildings. She showed Paula sections of the Ordnance Survey maps of the area. The large-scale maps are clear to read and easy to work from like the one below.

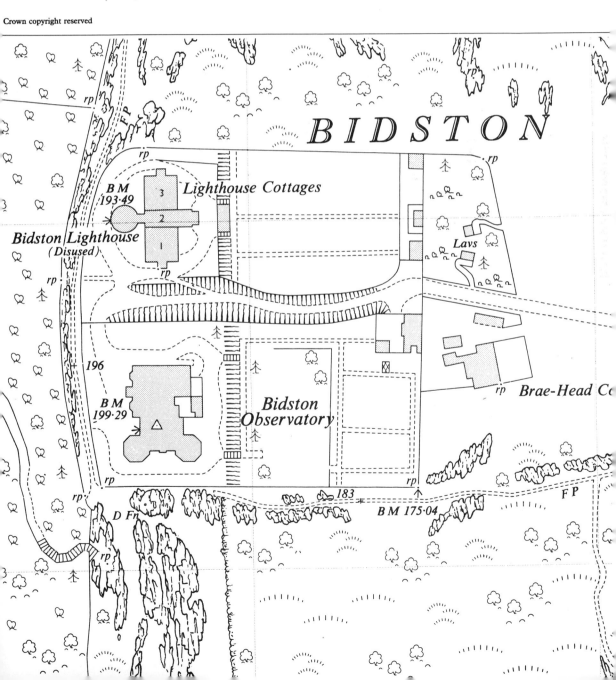

The children were puzzled to find a lighthouse so far from the sea. Look closely at the Ordnance Survey map on page 31 and at the old *engraving* of the Merseyside area.

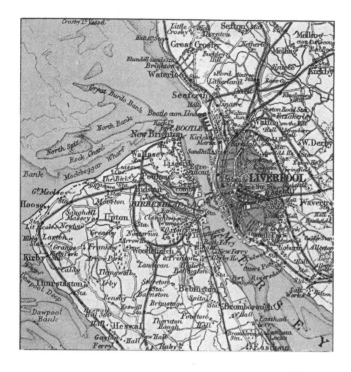

An old engraving

● Why do you think Bidston lighthouse is no longer used? (Clue: find out what a BM, or bench mark, shows.)

As they explored Bidston Hill, Paula and Colin discovered a number of round holes cut into the sandstone on the top. The librarian showed them the postcard seen below and explained that the holes were all that remained of a signalling system which was used over two hundred years ago.

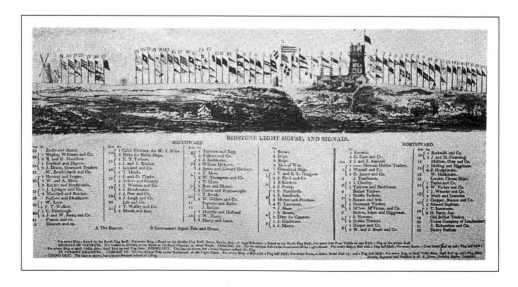

The ship owners and merchants in Liverpool knew that their ships were close to port when their flag was flown at the Bidston Signalling Station across the river Mersey.

- Why do you think the merchants needed to know when their ships were nearly home?

- Out of the fifty–eight flagpoles, forty–nine of them belonged to the shipowners and merchants. What do you think the other nine flagpoles were used for?

- Why do you think this method of signalling was not reliable?

The children drew their own plan of the top of the Bidston Hill, showing the remaining flagpole holes.

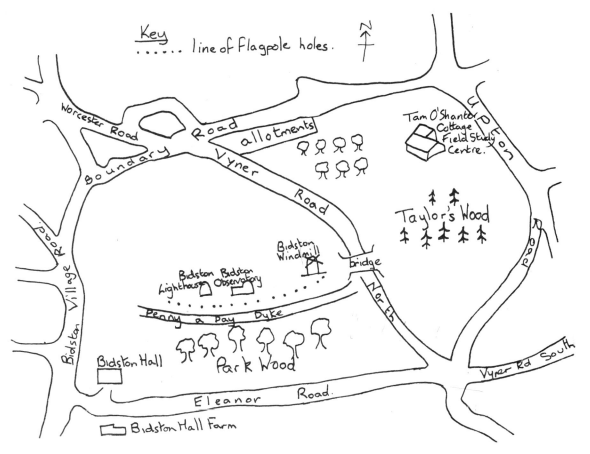

Bidston Observatory

Bidston Observatory

This large building is situated on Bidston Hill. Look for it on the Ordnance Survey section shown on page 31. From the local history records in the library the children were able to find out more details about the history and work of the Observatory.

Find out for yourself what kind of work is done in an Observatory.

The Observatory first opened in Liverpool in 1845 but moved across to Bidston in 1867. Why do you think this move became necessary? (The name of the building is a clue!)

Bidston Observatory is still very busy today. Paula and Colin were given a guided tour to see how new technology has changed the operations carried out in the building. Look up the word *seismology*. It will give you a clue to one of the things that is checked at the Observatory today.

● What new pieces of equipment do you think might be improving the work of the Observatory?

Bidston Mill

Colin and Paula can see the mill on top of Bidston Hill from their school playground. What type of mill is it? Why do you think it was built there?

Look back at the map on page 27. It shows the farms around Bidston village. What problems might these farmers have had taking their wheat to the mill?

A photo of the mill from the 1930s

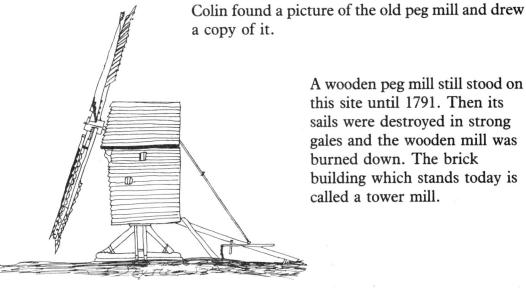

Colin found a picture of the old peg mill and drew a copy of it.

A wooden peg mill still stood on this site until 1791. Then its sails were destroyed in strong gales and the wooden mill was burned down. The brick building which stands today is called a tower mill.

● Find out the differences between *peg* and *tower* mills.

● How did they work?

Tam O'Shanter Field Centre

Tam O'Shanter Field Centre as it is today

Paula and Colin visited the Tam O'Shanter Field Centre on Bidston Hill as part of their project. Inside they found this old postcard showing the cottage as it was in the 1930s. Then it was a small farmstead with 6 acres of land.

Tam O'Shanter cottage in the 1930s

Look at this map based on Ordnance Survey showing Bidston Hill and the area surrounding it. Find Tam O'Shanter cottage. It is opposite Flaybrick Hill Cemetery.

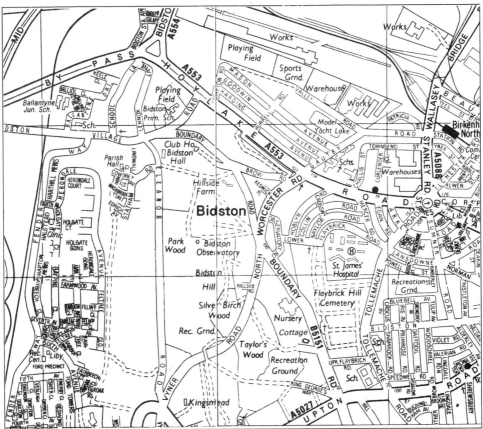

● Which wood is close to the cottage?

● What use do you think the farmer would have made of the wood?

● Do you think the farmer would have used the windmill on the Hill?

● Find out where the name *Tam O'Shanter* comes from.

Through the work of local groups and societies the Tam O'Shanter cottage was saved from demolition over ten years ago and converted into a Field Study Centre. Many people helped to raise money for the *renovation* work that needed doing and the local newspaper printed an article about it, an extract from which appears on the following page.

Part of our history is saved

BIRKENHEAD HISTORY SOCIETY is leading the fight to save Tam O'Shanter's ruined cottage on Bidston Hill from demolition. It is hoping to turn it into a field centre. The Society chairman said, 'We don't want to create a museum but a living, vibrant centre which will enhance Bidston Hill and the town of Birkenhead as a whole.'

The Society hope to raise £14,000 to do the renovation work. They are looking for any old photos of the cottage. As the chairman said, 'These photos will help our architects decide what the rebuilt building should look like.'

The age of the cottage is unknown but during renovation in 1953, a stone bearing the date 1511 was found.

The people planning the renovation work wanted to make the cottage look as it had originally.

- List the jobs and the types of craftsmen that would be needed.

- How would they collect the evidence so that they could build the cottage as it was?

- What materials which are not usually used today for housebuilding, do you think might be needed?

Is there an interesting or historical building near you which needs renovating? Try to find evidence of how it looked originally and make sketches to show this.

- Describe how you might raise the funds that would be needed.

Preservation or demolition?

Paula and Colin realised that not all of their classmates agreed that spending so much on a derelict old cottage was worthwhile. They therefore decided to invite someone who had been involved with the project to talk to the class and give them more information about the subject.

Mr Brown from the local Town Planning Department told the children that, 'We need memories, pieces of the past to help us to compose a picture of the present. It is impossible to 'freeze' history at any certain moment but it is possible to keep certain landmarks as evidence of the way that life is changing.'

To find out if your town has any *listed* buildings or *conservation areas*, ask at the local library. Go along to the planning department of your local council. They will have maps of the area and be able to tell you of any future plans to demolish buildings.

What can you do?

Following Mr Brown's advice, here is an action plan for you to follow. You can send out a letter like this to the people in your area.

```
Dear

We are searching for old buildings which can tell us something about the
history of our town.  With public interest and support, we might be able to keep
them so that everyone can enjoy them.

We hope that people will take a few minutes to stop and take a look around where
they live and decide which buildings are of interest.  If they are neglected you
might be able to help save them.  You can write to the local newspapers or
councillors, contact conservation groups and form local action groups.

We would be grateful if you would help us with our survey by completing the
enclosed questionnaire.
```

A copy of this questionnaire can accompany the letter.

```
   *  How long has your family lived in the area?

   *  Have you noticed much change in the town?

   *  Are you concerned that interesting old buildings
      are being demolished, or is it a waste of money
      to try and preserve them?

   *  Are there any derelict buildings in your area?

   *  Can you suggest any new uses for some of the
      derelict buildings?

   *  Are there any interesting buildings or objects
      in your area which you would like to see preserved?
```

A school in one area carried out their own local survey using the questions on page 39.

Here are some of the pupils' *conclusions*.

> * Are you concerned that interesting old buildings are being demolished, or is it a waste of money to try and preserve them?

Answer There was divided opinion on this question. Most people added remarks such as, "at reasonable cost" or "depends on the condition of the building." The majority were in favour of preservation but felt "not just because it is old, aesthetic values are main consideration."

> * Can you suggest any new uses for some of the derelict buildings?

Answer Numerous ideas. Suggestions were local History Museums, Marinas, shopping centres, cheap office accommodation, youth centres and art galleries.

From the replies the children persuaded the local council that there were several local buildings worth preserving for historical interest. The resulting publicity in local papers and television focusing on the neglect of disused canal buildings identified in the children's survey, led to the development of a canal museum on the site.

What do *you* think?

● Is it a waste of effort to try and save 'old buildings'?

● Are there any interesting old buildings near you?

● Do local people think they should be preserved?

● Could these buildings be used for something else?

New on old

Although Paula lives in a flat on a modern housing estate, she wanted to discover what had been on the land before. She knew that the Ford Estate had been built in the 1960s, so she looked for the 1959 Ordnance Survey map.

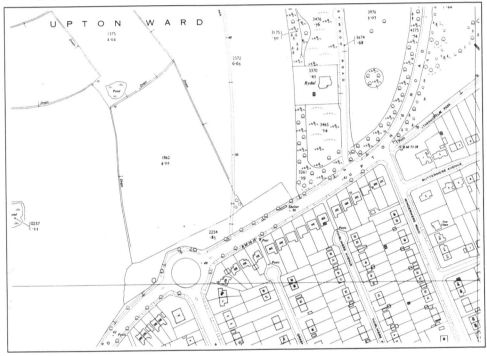

Here is a section which shows part of the land on which the Estate was later built. Look at the road plan on page 20. Find Upton Road on both maps. On the 1959 Ordnance Survey there are only fields stretching north of Upton Road, but on the later road plan you can see the maze of streets that now make up Paula's estate.

● Name the roads which form the boundaries of the estate.

● How many avenues are there?

● Do you notice anything unusual about the groups of street names around each avenue?

41

Old Birkenhead

Paula's parents had moved to the Ford Estate when it was built in 1967. They had been living with her grandparents in Park Road North, Birkenhead. Look at the Ordnance Survey map below. Find the junction of Park Road North and Duke Street. Paula's grandparents live in the corner house. Paula and Colin go to visit them every other Saturday.

- Draw a *linear* map to show the route that you think they might take. Start your journey at Bidston.

- List the long straight roads which lead into Birkenhead.

- Which road changes its name three times?

- From the evidence of the map where do all the major roads lead to? The old photo below gives you a clue.

Woodside Ferry in the 1930s

- How many different methods of transport are suggested in the picture?

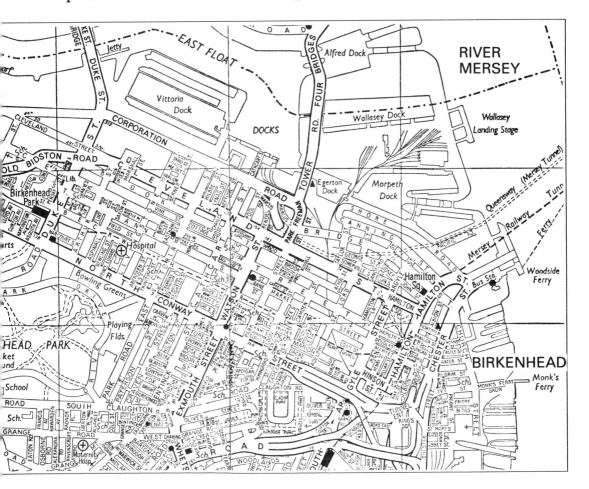

Mapping the growth of a town

Paula and Colin went looking in the library for more map evidence about how the town of Birkenhead had grown. They found these two maps which gave them some important information.

Look closely at the two maps.

- How long is the *time span* between them?

- Make a list of the changes in Birkenhead that you can find from studying the two maps.

- How do you think that life for the people in Birkenhead has been affected by these changes?

- Why do you think these changes took place? Look out for the clues given on the maps. The river Mersey is a big clue!

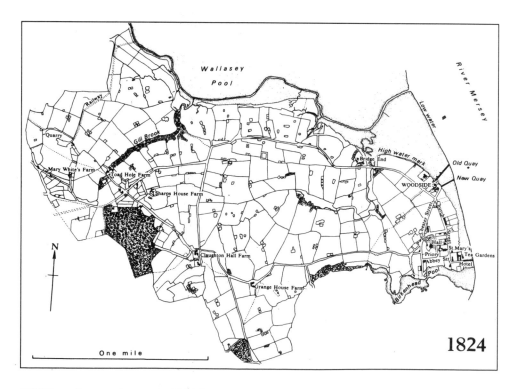

William Lawton's map of Birkenhead, 1824

- What is shown on the 1844 map on land belonging to Claughton Hall farm and Sharp's House farm?

- What clues can you spot which suggest different forms of transport by 1844?

- Look at the plan of the streets shown on the 1844 map. Find out what this *pattern* of streets is called. Look at a map of your town to find if there is a pattern to the street plan.

- How many ferries can you spot? Where are they going? (Clue: look at the photograph on page 43.)

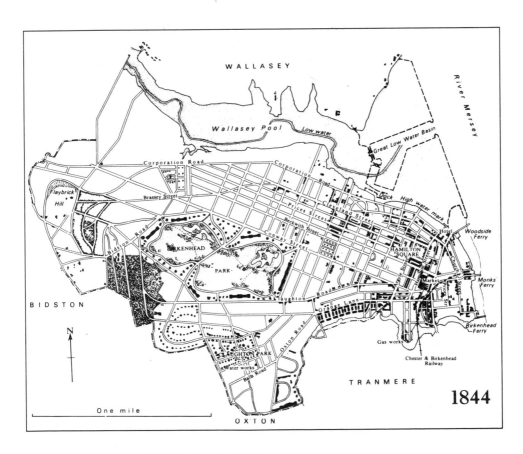

James Law's map of Birkenhead, 1844

Birkenhead docks

Another kind of map which has been mentioned on page 8 is the *aerial photograph*. Paula found this one of Birkenhead docks which had been taken in the 1930s. Look back at the map on pages 42–43. The three parallel roads in the background of the photograph are Price Street, Cleveland Street and Corporation Road. Can you see which dock runs alongside them?

A PORTION OF THE MERSEY DOCK ESTATE AT BIRKENHEAD

The photograph show how busy the docks were at that time. The photograph below shows an area of Birkenhead dockland today.

● What differences do you notice? Why do you think this is?

Paula's grandfather remembers the days when the docks were busy:

'It's sad to see the docks now. No ships in, everywhere empty. When I worked here it was hustle and bustle everyday with ships to unload and new cargo to store.

At one time there were so many different nations' flags flying here from ships that it made you dizzy counting the different countries.'

Doing it yourself

If like Paula and Colin you decide to explore the area in which you live through maps, here are some *sources* to help you get started.

1 In the local collection at your library or *County Record Office*, you should be able to find the early maps drawn for your area. Maps drawn before the end of the seventeenth century are not very accurate and usually do not have roads marked on them.

2 Your County Record Office should have a copy of the *tithe map* for your local area.

3 Ordnance Survey maps of your local area are available in most book shops. They are always being redrawn and reissued. The larger scale ones, 1:25,000, are ideal for studying areas in detail.

4 Your local librarian will know where aerial photographs of your area can be seen.

You will find your local librarian a great help in searching for evidence through maps. The librarian will be able to suggest which scale of map to use to show the detail that you will need to see.

Working with maps is fun. You will be surprised at how quickly you can become familiar with the way to use maps to discover evidence about the history of your area.

INDEX

ACKNOWLEDGEMENTS

The author and publishers wish to thank Trudy Boyle for help with research and layout, the staff at Neston Library and the following for permission to reproduce material:

Geographers' A–Z Map Co. Ltd. **pp 20, 37**; Bob Bird **cover, pp 26, 29, 34, 36** (top), **46** (bottom); Ian and Marilyn Boumphrey *"Yesterday's Wirral – Birkenhead, Prenton & Oxton"* **pp 21, 25, 30, 32** (×2), **35, 36** (bottom), **43, 46** (top); Cheshire County Council **p4**; Cheshire Record Office **p6**; County of Shropshire Cartographic Services **p8**; Nance Fyson **p16**; Ordnance Survey maps reproduced with the permission of the Controller of Her Majesty's Stationery Office, Crown copyright reserved **cover, pp 7, 14, 15, 17, 24, 27, 31, 37, 41, 42–3** (scale 1:25,000 – p 7; 1:1250 – pp 17, 24, 27, 31, 41)

Artwork by John Booth **pp 26, 28**

Cover by Chi Leung

Designed by Jenny Clouter